MEETING GOD BIBLE STUDIES

MEETING
GOD IN
PRAISE

Juanita Ryan

*6 studies for individuals
or groups*

InterVarsity Press
Downers Grove, Illinois

InterVarsity Press
P.O. Box 1400, Downers Grove, IL 60515

©1999 by InterVarsity Christian Fellowship/USA

InterVarsity Press® is the book-publishing division of InterVarsity Christian Fellowship/USA®, a student movement active on campus at hundreds of universities, colleges and schools of nursing in the United States of America, and a member movement of the International Fellowship of Evangelical Students. For information about local and regional activities, write Public Relations Dept., InterVarsity Christian Fellowship/USA, 6400 Schroeder Rd., P.O. Box 7895, Madison, WI 53707-7895.

All Scripture quotations, unless otherwise indicated, are taken from the Holy Bible, New International Version®. NIV®. *Copyright ©1973, 1978, 1984 by International Bible Society. Used by permission of Zondervan Publishing House. All rights reserved.*

Cover illustration: Roberta Polfus

ISBN 0-8308-2055-8

Printed in the United States of America

Contents

Contents

INTRODUCING
Meeting God in Praise

I have often had friends and counseling clients tell me that they received little, if any, praise from their parents because their parents were afraid praise would make them conceited. In this way of thinking, praise is something we do to stroke someone else's ego.

Some of us may think of praising God as something we do to stroke his ego. This is actually closely related to the rather primitive idea that we need to appease God; that we need to keep him happy by making him feel good about himself. This idea inherently includes the thought that we need to grovel before God as we praise him. We stroke God and put ourselves down. If this is how we think of praise in relation to God, we will meet a puny, tyrannical god in our times of praise.

The kind of praise the God of Scripture calls us to is very different from this. It is a praise that involves remembering who God is, expressing our gratitude to him as a way of taking in his goodness and love for us more fully, singing a love song to him as we delight in him, and joining our hearts, minds and spirits to him in a oneness that brings a deep and satisfying joy. This kind of praise leads us into the presence of the true and living God who lifts us out of our worst fears about ourselves and calls us his children. We are not stroking an ego and groveling, we are celebrating God's love for us and our love for God.

Praise is remembering who God is. It allows us to focus again on God. In the midst of life we can lose our focus and forget who God is in his greatness and power and in his intimate love. As we praise God, we remember and regain perspective not only about God but about ourselves and our lives.

Praise is also an expression of our gratitude for God's good gifts to us. We have learned to say thank-you out of politeness. But saying thank-you is far more significant than following a rule of etiquette, especially when it comes to expressing our gratitude to God. Such expressions help us to take in more fully God's attentive, caring presence in our lives. Praise in this sense helps us to be more deeply transformed by his good gifts to us.

When two people love each other deeply they express their love in words. They say "I love you," and then they might list some of the specific ways they find themselves delighting in the other person. Our relationship with God is a love relationship. Praise is a song of love and delight which we sing to the Lover of our souls.

Finally, praise is a joining of our hearts and minds and spirits to this One who loves us now and always. We are surrendering our lives to him. We are joining our spirit to his Spirit in a praise that moves us beyond words into the reality of everyday life so that the ordinary acts of living become our praise.

The practice of spiritual disciplines can assist you to praise God in these ways—remembering who God is, expressing your gratitude for him, singing songs of love to him, and joining your heart, mind and spirit to him so that you are one with him. The following studies are designed to lead you through a series of spiritual disciplines with the focus on meeting God in praise.

Practicing the Disciplines

Each of the studies focuses on a different spiritual discipline that takes us deeper into the topic.

1. *Scripture study:* we begin with an inductive study that reveals what the Bible has to say about the topic.

2. *Confession:* we look at ourselves in light of Scripture, taking time in the midst of Bible study for silent reflection and repentance.

3. *Community:* we move to interaction with others around a passage or an exercise, asking for guidance and encouragement as we seek God.

4. *Silence:* again we come before Scripture, but this time seeking not to analyze but to hear God's voice and guidance for us.

5. *Obedience:* in light of Scripture's teaching we make commitments to change.

6. *Prayer:* we take time to seek God, weaving prayer through our encounter with Scripture.

These sessions are designed to be completed in 45 minutes to an hour in a group or 30 minutes in personal study. However, feel free to follow the leading of the Holy Spirit and spend as long as is needed on each study.

Every session has several components.

Turning Toward God. Discussion or reflection questions and exercises to draw us into the topic at hand.

Receiving God's Word. A Bible study with application and spiritual exercises.

Now or Later. Ideas that can be used at the end of the study as a time of quiet for a group or individual. Or these ideas can be used between studies in quiet times.

The components of this guide can help us meet God with both our minds and hearts. May your times of praise be times of meeting the true and living God in ways that enrich and transform your life.

1

PRAISE FOR GOD'S PROMISE

······································

The Discipline
of Scripture Study

God is a God of promises. Scripture is full of his promises to us. Promises of blessing, of hope, of wonderful gifts. When we hear God's promises and believe his Word to us, we cannot help but respond with gratitude and praise. In the anticipatory praise that comes from reflecting on his promises to us, we join our spirits to God's and meet him in ever-deepening ways.

TURNING TOWARD GOD *Picture yourself as a child. An adult you know and trust to be true to his word has promised you what you have always hoped for—a week camping in the woods or a trip to Disneyworld (you fill in the details).

*What response would you have to this promise?

*What response would you have toward the person making the promise?

The Discipline of Scripture Study

God's Word is one of our greatest resources for knowing him and drawing close to him. What follows is an inductive Bible study that will help you draw out the truths of Scripture for yourself through three types of questions: observation (to gather the facts), interpretation (to discern the meaning) and application (to relate the truths of Scripture to our lives).

 RECEIVING GOD'S WORD   1. Read Jeremiah 31:3-14. How would you describe the relationship between God and his people from these verses?

2. What specific promises does God make?

3. What is significant about what God says about his love in verse 3?

4. What responses does God say the people will have when his promises are realized in verses 9 and 12?

5. Put yourself in the peoples' place. What would it be like for you to hear these promises?

6. What would it be like to see these promises fulfilled?

7. Reflect on some of the promises made in Scripture that you have seen fulfilled in your own life. Write about one or two of them.

8. What responses do you have as you reflect on these promises and on the way they were fulfilled in your life?

9. What is the prophet calling the people to do in verse 7 and why?

10. What are some of your favorite ways of praising God?

11. What is your experience of God when you praise him in these ways?

Thank God for his promises to you.

 NOW OR LATER Each day this week spend a few minutes focusing on one of God's promises to you. Write a prayer of praise for each promise you reflect on throughout the week.

2

PRAISE FOR FORGIVENESS

Practicing the
Discipline of Confession

Forgiveness is one of God's most astonishing gifts to us. It is a gift that offers us freedom, wholeness and hope. It is a gift that shows us God's tender compassion and mercy toward us when we fail and when we fall. He is always ready and eager to have us receive his outstretched hand so he can lift us up and set us on our way again. All we have to do is speak our need and take his hand. Its called *confession*.

 TURNING TOWARD GOD *Recall a time in the past when you sought and received God's forgiveness. What thoughts and feelings do you have about God as you remember this experience?

*Does asking for forgiveness come easily for you? Explain.

The Discipline of Confession

God calls us to honesty—honesty with ourselves, with him and with each other. He does not want us to be defensive or blind but to be open to him so he can teach us to love as he loves. Confession is an opportunity to tell the truth about the ways we have hurt ourselves and others and turned from God's way of love. It is an opportunity to open our hearts and minds to God's Spirit to correct and change us. It is an opportunity to make different, more loving and godly choices each day, one day at a time.

 RECEIVING GOD'S WORD   1. Read Hosea 14. How would you summarize the first three verses of this text in which the people are called to confession?

2. How would you rewrite this call, making it contemporary?

3. What is God's response (vv. 4-8)?

4. List the metaphors of healing in verses 5-8.

5. Choose one of these metaphors and in a time of quiet allow yourself to reflect on it. What thoughts came to mind?

6. What does this metaphor tell you about who God is?

7. How might this metaphor of God's forgiveness strengthen you to prepare yourself for confession?

8. Spend some time in quiet reflection and confession. Acknowledge any hurtful thoughts or behaviors to God. Ask God to bring to your mind other thoughts or behaviors he wants to change in you.

9. Picture God responding to you as he responds in the text.

10. What thoughts and feelings do you have as you see God responding to you in this way?

11. How would you summarize the last verse of the chapter?

12. What is God saying to you specifically at this time about walking in his ways?

Thank God for the forgiveness he offers you.

 NOW OR LATER   Spend some time each day reflecting on the metaphors from this text. Journal your thoughts and feelings in response to God's forgiveness.

3

PRAISE FOR CHRIST'S BODY

·····

Practicing the Discipline of Community

A listening ear. An affirmation. A meal. A hug. A prayer. A caring presence. A hand to hold. A joining in celebration. A deep friendship. These are some of the many gifts we receive from other believers who know Jesus and who speak his words of love and grace to us as they also seek to "walk in love" as Jesus taught. These are precious gifts of Christ's presence with us in others. In our gratitude and praise for this gift, may our capacity to meet God in these ways be enlarged.

The Discipline of Community

We were created for relationship with God and with each other. God created us with a need for community. It is in community that we experience love and are given the opportunity to express love. It is in community that we see where our rough edges are and where God is at work in our lives. It is in community that we grow into deeper maturity in Christ. The following exercises and Scripture study are designed to be done with one or two others or in a small group. Ask someone you trust to work through this material with you.

 TURNING TOWARD GOD   *Share a favorite memory of a fun or funny experience from your church life with one another.

*In a time of prayer together, ask God to remind you of ways you have been loved and cared for by other members of Christ's body.

*Take some time to tell each other stories of how you have been cared for by those in your church family.

 RECEIVING GOD'S WORD   **1.** Read Ephesians 5:8-21. What does Paul, the author, say about the benefits of living in the light?

2. The source of light in our lives is Christ (v. 14). In verses 8-18 what choices does Paul encourage us to make in order to continue to live in the light?

3. How does living in the light affect our relationships (vv. 14-21)?

4. How have you personally experienced the impact on your relationships of living in God's light?

5. Verses 19 and 20 call us into relationship with each other and with God. What does Paul encourage us to do in relationship with each other?

in relationship with God?

6. In your experience what is the value of worshiping, singing, praising and giving thanks in community?

7. How does it affect your relationship with those you worship with?

8. How does it affect your relationship with God?

9. How would you paraphrase verse 21?

Give examples of what this might look like in relation to your worship.

10. In a time of quiet reflection, ask God to show you what he is saying to you through these verses.

11. How has sharing your reflections on this text with your group or with a companion enriched your experience of this study?

Praise God for his many gifts in those who are Christ in the flesh to you.

 NOW OR LATER   Make it a goal this week to verbalize your gratitude to others for who they are to you.

4

PRAISE FOR THE SPIRIT

....

Practicing the Discipline of Silence

God's Spirit is an intimate presence living in us; the transcendent God, making his home with us. The Spirit offers himself as Guide, Teacher, Counselor, Comforter, Helper. As we daily give our lives to him, he leads us in the Father's good and loving will for our lives and makes us more and more like Jesus. Such a gift deserves our highest praise.

The Discipline of Silence

For many of us the disciplines of silence and meditation are the most difficult to pursue. We want to complete a task—read through a book of the Bible or pray through a list of needs. Sometimes, however, God wants us to simply come before him and wait to hear his voice. The reflection and Bible study here are best done in quiet, whether you are in a room with others in your small group or alone. Complete all of the questions on your own, then, if you choose, discuss them with a group.

TURNING TOWARD GOD *In a time of quiet, reflect on God's Spirit. How do you think and feel about this person of the Trinity?

*Spend some time in praise and gratitude, thanking the Spirit for his presence in your life.

 RECEIVING GOD'S WORD
1. Read John 14:16-18 several times.

[16]I will ask the Father, and he will give you another Counselor to be with you forever—[17]the Spirit of truth. The world cannot accept him, because it neither sees him or knows him. But you know him, for he lives with you and will be in you. [18]I will not leave you as orphans; I will come to you.

2. Pray for God to guide you to the verse or phrase he wants to use to speak to you.

3. Read the passage again slowly, taking time with each phrase.

4. Notice all that the passage says about the Spirit.

5. Invite the Spirit of God to be with you at this time.

6. What responses do you have as you read the words of this passage and listen to the Spirit?

7. What message does God have for you today?

8. Write a response, expressing praise for the gift of God's Spirit.

Allow whatever you have experienced of God in this time to fill you with joy. Offer your thanks to God.

NOW OR LATER   God's Spirit is known to us as Teacher (John 16:12-13), Counselor (John 15:26) and Helper (Romans 8:26-27). Each day this week focus on one of these functions and how it has been significant to you personally. Conclude this time of reflection by writing a prayer of praise to the Spirit.

5

PRAISE FOR GOD'S GUIDANCE

....

Practicing the
Discipline of Obedience

We all have a strong sense that life has some hidden purpose and meaning, and that our unique life has some unique purpose. We find ourselves looking at life events and asking what they mean, what purpose they serve, what we were meant to learn from them. Without some sense of purpose we may feel that we have no value and that we are just going through pointless motions.

Scripture confirms our deep sense that our lives have meaning. Scripture also teaches us that the discovery of that meaning is an unfolding process which happens as we seek and follow God's guidance in our lives—in all the big and little turning points we face. Understanding this can bring a deeper joy to practicing the discipline of obedience.

 TURNING TOWARD GOD   *Think of a time when you specifically sought and received God's guidance. What was the experience like for you?

*What did you discover about God from the experience?

*What did you discover about yourself?

The Discipline of Obedience
Like a good and loving parent, God wants us to stay close by his side so he can guide and teach and care for us. He wants us to walk with him in his way of love so we can know life's deepest joys. This is the call to obedience. As we practice the discipline of obedience and watch God's will unfold in our lives, we will grow in our trust of God's tremendous love for us, and our desire to continue this discipline will grow even stronger.

 RECEIVING GOD'S WORD   1. Read Psalm 119:9-16. How would you describe the psalmist's feelings and desires about his relationship with God?

2. What does he ask of God (vv. 10, 12)?

3. What basic wisdom does he set out in verse 9?

4. What actions does he take to follow the wisdom of verse 9 (vv. 10-16)?

5. How might these actions help him in his quest to obey God?

6. How have you found one of these actions especially helpful in your life?

7. Spend a few minutes in quiet reflection. Which of these actions might be especially important for you to follow in the next week?

8. Plan a way to make this a part of your life this next week.

9. Again in a time of quiet, ask God to show you what guidance he wants to give you at this time.

10. Write a prayer of praise, thanking God for his guidance and asking for the strength to do his will.

Thank God for his guidance in your life.

NOW OR LATER   Begin each day asking that God's loving will would be done in your life. Ask for his guidance throughout the day in all that you do and think. At the end of each day journal your experience of God's guidance and help.

6

PRAISE FOR GOD

Practicing the Discipline of Prayer

Prayer is simply talking with God. We may be talking to him about our needs or about the needs of others. We may be confessing our sin or asking for guidance. We may be giving him our lives and wills. We may be saying thank you. But in all these things prayer is always a love song. From our experiences of God in the intimacy of prayer, flows our deepest praise—our songs of love to him for who he is and all he does.

 TURNING TOWARD GOD   *Think about some of your favorite love songs. What are some of the phrases you especially like?

*How could some of these phrases be used in a song of love to God?

*God also sings love songs to us. In a time of quiet ask God to help you hear his song of love to you.

*What thoughts and feelings did you have as you listened for God's song of love for you?

The Discipline of Prayer

Prayer is an opportunity to draw close to God. In prayer we can express our gratitude, tell him our needs, release our fears and listen for his voice. We may not always feel that we have connected with God, but as we remain faithful to seeking him and listening to him, we will experience the riches of companionship with God.

 RECEIVING GOD'S WORD   **1.** Read Psalm 147:1-11. What title would you give to this passage?

2. List all the actions the psalmist praises God for.

3. List all the qualities of character the psalmist praises God for.

4. When you look at God's actions and qualities in this way, what thoughts and feelings do you have toward God?

5. What actions of God do you want to praise him for?

6. What qualities of character do you want to praise God for?

7. Take some time to write and reflect. What would you like to say to God about your love for him?

8. Using your responses to the last three questions, put together a psalm of your own.

9. What would you like to do to praise God?

Thank God for who he is.

 NOW OR LATER   Spend time each day praising God for who he is. Each day find a new way to express this praise—in writing, in song, in saying, "I love you," or in whatever way you choose.

Guidelines for Leaders

My grace is sufficient for you. (2 Corinthians 12:9)

If leading a small group is something new for you, don't worry. These sessions are designed to be led easily. As a matter of fact, the flow of questions in the Bible study portions through the passage from observation to interpretation to application is so natural that you may feel that the studies lead themselves.

You don't need to be an expert on the Bible or a trained teacher to lead a small group discussion. The idea behind these sessions is that the leader guides group members to discover for themselves what the Bible has to say and to listen for God's guidance. This method of learning will allow group members to remember much more of what is said than a lecture would.

This study guide is flexible. You can use it with a variety of groups—student, professional, neighborhood or church groups. Each study takes forty-five to sixty minutes in a group setting.

There are some important facts to know about group dynamics and encouraging discussion. The suggestions listed below should enable you to effectively and enjoyably fulfill your role as leader.

Preparing for the Study

1. Ask God to help you understand and apply the passage in your own life. Unless this happens, you will not be prepared to lead others. Pray too for the various members of the group. Ask God to open your hearts to the message of his Word and motivate you to action.

2. Read the introduction to the entire guide to get an overview of the issues which will be explored.

3. As you begin each study, read and reread the assigned Bible passage to familiarize yourself with it.

4. This study guide is based on the New International Version of the Bible. It will help you and the group if you use this translation as the basis for your study and discussion.

5. Carefully work through each question in the study. Spend time in meditation and reflection as you consider how to respond.

6. Write your thoughts and responses in the space provided in the study guide. This will help you to express your understanding of the passage clearly.

7. It might help to have a Bible dictionary handy. Use it to look up any unfamiliar words, names or places. (For additional help on how to study a passage, see chapter five of *Leading Bible Discussions*, InterVarsity Press.)

8. Consider how you need to apply the Scripture to your life. Remember that the group will follow your lead in responding to the studies. They will not go any deeper than you do.

Leading the Study

1. Begin the study on time. Open with prayer, asking God to help the group to understand and apply the passage.

2. Be sure that everyone in your group has a study guide. There are some questions and activities they will need to work through on their own—either beforehand or during the study session.

3. The flow of each study varies a bit. Many of the studies have time for silent reflection as well as for group discussion. Think through how you will lead the groups through the times of silence, and read through the notes for guidance. It can be very powerful to have times of silence in the midst of a group session. Session four

focuses on silence particularly and calls for an extended time apart. Then you can come together and share your experiences.

4. At the beginning of your first time together, explain that these studies are meant to be discussions, not lectures. Encourage the members of the group to participate. However, do not put pressure on those who may be hesitant to speak during the first few sessions. You may want to suggest the following guidelines to your group.

☐ Stick to the topic being discussed.

☐ Your responses should be based on the verses that are the focus of the discussion and not on outside authorities such as commentaries or speakers.

☐ These studies focus on a particular passage of Scripture. Only rarely should you refer to other portions of the Bible. This allows for everyone to participate on equal ground and for in-depth study.

☐ Anything said in the group is considered confidential and will not be discussed outside the group unless specific permission is given to do so.

☐ Provide time for each person present to talk if he or she feels comfortable doing so.

☐ Listen attentively to each other and learn from one another.

☐ Pray for each other.

5. Have a group member read the introduction at the beginning of the discussion.

6. Every session begins with the "Turning Toward God" section. The questions or activities are meant to be used before the passage is read. These questions introduce the theme of the study and encourage group members to begin to open up. Encourage as many members as possible to participate, and be ready to get the discussion going with your own response.

7. Either prior to or right after "Turning Toward God" you will see a definition of the specific discipline the session focuses on.

Have someone read that explanation.

8. Have one or more group member(s) read aloud the passage to be studied.

9. As you ask the questions under "Receiving God's Word," keep in mind that they are designed to be used just as they are written. You may simply read them aloud. Or you may prefer to express them in your own words.

There may be times when it is appropriate to deviate from the study guide. For example, a question may have already been answered. If so, move on to the next question. Or someone may raise an important question not covered in the guide. Take time to discuss it, but try to keep the group from going off on tangents.

10. Avoid answering your own questions. If necessary, repeat or rephrase them until they are clearly understood. Or point out something you read in the leader's notes to clarify the context or meaning. An eager group quickly becomes passive and silent if they think the leader will do most of the talking.

11. Don't be afraid of silence in response to the discussion questions. People may need time to think about the question before formulating their answers.

12. Don't be content with just one answer. Ask, "What do the rest of you think?" or "Anything else?" until several people have given answers to the question.

13. Acknowledge all contributions. Try to be affirming whenever possible. Never reject an answer. If it is clearly off-base, ask, "Which verse led you to that conclusion?" or again, "What do the rest of you think?"

14. Don't expect every answer to be addressed to you, even though this will probably happen at first. As group members become more at ease, they will begin to truly interact with each other. This is one sign of healthy discussion.

15. Don't be afraid of controversy. It can be very stimulating. If you don't resolve an issue completely, don't be frustrated. Move on and keep it in mind for later. A subsequent study may solve the problem.

16. Periodically summarize what the group has said about the passage. This helps to draw together the various ideas mentioned and gives continuity to the study. But don't preach.

17. At the end of the Bible discussion you may want to allow group members a time of quiet to work on an idea under "Now or Later." Then discuss what you experienced. Or you may want to encourage group members to work on these ideas between meetings. Give an opportunity during the session to allow people to talk about what they are learning.

18. Conclude your time together with conversational prayer, adapting the prayer suggestion at the end of the study to your group. Ask for God's help in following through on the commitments you've made.

19. End on time.

Many more suggestions and helps are found in *Small Group Leader's Handbook* and *The Big Book on Small Groups* (both from InterVarsity Press). Reading through one of these books would be worth your time.

Study Notes

Study 1. Praise for God's Promise. Jeremiah 31:3-14.
Purpose: To reflect on the promises of God through the discipline of Scripture study.

Question 1. Encourage participants to share whatever strikes them as they look at this text from a broad perspective. The relationship described here between God and his people is that of a relationship that is being restored. God is intimately loving, generous in his promises, making powerful promises to the people of Israel.

Question 2. The nation of Israel has been living in captivity. The promise God made to Abraham and his descendants that he would give them a home where he would dwell with them seems like a fantasy of the past. Now, through the prophet Jeremiah, God is telling his people that he will restore them as a people to their home, and most significantly, to himself. The images of this text are images of abundant blessing, celebration, healing and joy.

It can be a powerful exercise as a group to name the many promises God makes in this text. God's promises include: "I will build you up again and you will be rebuilt" (v. 4); you will dance and celebrate (v. 4); "you will plant vineyards . . . and enjoy their fruit" (v. 5, this is a metaphor for living long and in security in one place—for returning home and living there); I will gather you from all the places you have been scattered (v. 8); I will lead you and provide for you (streams and a level path, v. 9); I will redeem you from those stronger than you (v. 11); you will shout for joy (v. 12); you will enjoy abundance (v. 12); you will not be sad (v. 12); you "will dance and be glad" (v. 13); you will know "comfort and joy instead of sorrow" (v. 13); you will be satisfied and filled with the abundance of my good gifts to you (v. 14).

Question 3. God declares his love to his people. He tells them he loves them with an everlasting love—a love that always is. Even in the hard times of exile, God loves them.

Question 4. Verse 9 tells us that the people will come back weeping and praying. Verse 12 tells us that when they reach Zion (the holy city) they will shout for joy. This is a deeply emotional experience. Any time we experience restoration in our relationship with God, we are likely to weep in grief for the loss and pain we have suffered, to weep in longing, and to weep in gratitude. All of this and more we express to God in prayer. But the weeping gives way to shouts of joy as we experience ourselves in God's presence, in his arms of love.

Question 5. Your group members may have a variety of reactions to picturing themselves hearing these promises. Some may realize that they would feel skeptical. Some may realize they would want to believe such good news but be afraid to trust it. Others might respond with feelings of hopefulness and gratitude.

Question 6. Seeing such glorious promises fulfilled will likely fill us with awe and gratitude. There may be some who realize they would struggle to receive such good gifts, however. Old wounds may leave them believing they do not deserve good things or that they cannot trust love to be real or to last.

Questions 7-8. Allow a time of silence for people to write and reflect on question 7. If some in the group are new to Scripture, they may reflect on ways they have seen God provide for them in the past. Then follow up with question 8. Some may also want to tell the specifics of how they've see God's promises fulfilled in their lives.

Question 9. The prophet calls the people to come together in the place of worship so they can praise God by singing with joy, shouting and making their praises heard.

Questions 10-11. Encourage participants to share their experiences of praising God. Allow for a variety of experiences and expression.

Study 2. Praise for Forgiveness. Hosea 14.

Purpose: To experience forgiveness through the discipline of confession, praising God for this extraordinary gift.

Turning Toward God. Allow a time of silent reflection. Then follow up with the question to allow people to discuss their experiences.

Question 1. You can expect that participants will summarize this call to confession in different ways, depending on the aspects of the verses that struck them most.

The call to confession includes a number of actions: return to God; take words of confession with you; acknowledge the folly of trying to depend on yourself rather than on God, believing in your own power rather than God's, remember who God is—a God of compassion and understanding.

Question 2. You may want to give a few minutes for people to write out their own wording, and then discuss it together.

Question 3. God's response to the people's confession is generous, loving, extravagant, powerful, healing, forgiving, life-giving.

Questions 4-7. The metaphors take the people from forgiveness to healing—to new life which is flourishing, thriving, blossoming. To return to God, to confess our sins and to acknowledge our moment-by-moment need of God is to invite God's life to flourish in us. The images of this gift of new life include: a lily blossoming; a cedar of Lebanon sending down roots and growing and providing shade; a grapevine blossoming and providing award-winning wine. Also included are images of God as the dew on the lily and as a green pinetree—the source of our life and fruitfulness.

The purpose of these questions is to allow people to talk about the discipline of confession and how they experience God's forgiveness. Some may want to mention specific instances of sin or confession, but this is not the goal.

Questions 8-10. Allow time alone for responses to these questions—at least ten minutes. Invite members to share their experience of this time as they feel comfortable. If you and the group want to, you may agree ahead of time to come back together but not discuss your experiences (as a way to respect each person's privacy with God). Either way, it would be good to have a group member read a verse out loud, such as 1 John 1:9, as a way of reminding participants that they are forgiven.

Questions 11-12. The last verse is a call to wisdom, a call that echoes the opening call. The text begins by calling us to return to God, realizing that we have foolishly tried to live by our own power without him. The last verse calls us to continue this new way of life. Having returned to God, the wise choice for us is to stay with him, to walk with him, to acknowledge that he is God, to depend on him, to follow his ways. Encourage group participants to reflect specifically on what God is directing them to do or to be at this time.

Study 3. Praise for Christ's Body. Ephesians 5:8-21.

Purpose: To praise God for his body and experience God's gift of community.

Question 1. Paul says that we are now "light in the Lord." He goes on to say that living in God's light results in goodness, righteousness and truth.

Question 2. Paul encourages us to make wise choices—all of which are a part of waking up from sleep, being awake and alive, and living in God's light (v. 14). These choices include: seeking God's will (v.

10), seeing life's events as opportunities (v. 16), not getting drunk (numbing ourselves so that we are less aware of our choices and behaviors, v. 18) and opening ourselves to God's Spirit (v. 18).

Question 3. Living in God's light brings honesty (vv. 9-14), intimacy (v. 19) and humility (v. 21) to our relationships.

Question 4. Think of specific ways you have seen your relationship with God influence your relationships with others.

Questions 5-8. Verses 19-20 are a call to worship and praise in community. Reflect personally and specifically on your experience of community and your experience of God in the midst of praise.

Question 9. Submitting to each other out of reverence for Christ is a picture of relating to each other as if we were relating to Christ himself, because Christ lives in us and in the other person. It is a picture of respectful, humble relating.

Question 10. Give participants time to reflect on the text and their exploration of it, asking for specific guidance from God about ways he wants to challenge, correct, encourage or enlighten them. If the group is comfortable with sharing their sense of God's leading at this time, give time to do this.

Study 4. Praise for the Spirit. John 14:16-18.
Purpose: To discover through the discipline of silence the joy of knowing God's presence in praise.

The questions in this study are especially meant for a time of silence and solitude. If you are leading a group, help people get into the right frame of mind by singing or listening to a couple worship songs together. Have someone read the introduction and the explanation of the discipline of silence.

Before you read the text, set the context for these verses. Jesus is saying his goodbyes to his disciples just before his death. Jesus is telling his disciples he must leave them soon, but he promises them the Spirit. Then read the passage aloud.

Encourage people to find a private place. Allow about 45 minutes for people to write in response to the questions and to sit in silence, listening to God and reflecting on God.

If the group chooses to share some of what they experienced during the time of silence, allow time to do so when you regather. Close in prayer together.

Study 5. Praise for God's Guidance. Psalm 119:9-16.

Purpose: To experience God's guidance through the discipline of obedience.

Question 1. The purpose of this question is to draw people into the text and to give an overview of the text. The psalmist has a deep longing for God and a deep longing to follow God's ways.

Question 3. Verse 9 provides the foundation for this text. The wisdom found in verse 9 is that we cannot live a pure life without God. We need God's instruction, guidance and Word to teach us and to make this possible.

Question 4. The actions the psalmist takes are: he seeks God with all his heart (v. 10); he has taken God's word into his heart and life (v. 11); he praises God (v. 12); he recounts what God has said (v. 13); he rejoices in following God's statues as one rejoices in great riches (v. 14); he meditates on God's precepts (v. 15); he reflects on God's ways (v. 15); he does not neglect God's word (v. 16).

Question 5. These actions describe a process of being deeply engaged emotionally, mentally and spiritually with the pursuit of God and his ways—paying attention, giving oneself to this, valuing God's ways, and rejoicing in being able to follow God's ways.

Question 6. Describe how you have done some of what the psalmist describes, making it as specific and personal as possible and describing its impact on your life. Sharing in this way can encourage a sense of new, creative possibilities in pursuing God.

Questions 7-9. Give people time to respond individually to these questions. After about ten minutes of private reflection, invite them to share what they want to of how they sense God speaking to them or directing them at this time.

Question 10. Allow time to write your prayers. You may want to read these prayers out loud as a way of closing your time together.

Study 6. Praise for God. Psalm 147:1-11.

Purpose: To meet God in the practice of the discipline of prayer.

Turning Toward God. If appropriate to your group, you could create and sing an actual love song for God.

Question 1. The purpose of this question is to give an overview of the passage. Encourage a variety of responses.

Question 2. This question focuses on the actions of God that the psalmist describes. The Lord "builds up Jerusalem" and gathers the exiles (v. 2), "heals the brokenhearted and binds up their wounds" (v. 3), "determines the number of stars and calls them each by name," (v. 4), "sustains the humble but casts the wicked to the ground" (v. 6), "covers the sky with clouds . . . supplies the earth with rain and makes grass grow" (v. 8), "provides food for the cattle and for the young ravens" (v. 9).

Question 3. The qualities of God's character that the psalmist praises God for include: God is great and mighty in power (v. 5); God's understanding has no limit (v. 5); God's love is unfailing (v. 11); God delights in our trust in his love (v. 11).

Question 4. The psalmist shows us God's majestic power and his intimate, tender love. He shows us his activity and personal involvement in all of creation, from providing for the young raven to naming and knowing each star, to delighting in our hope and trust in him. Allow people to express whatever thoughts and feelings they may have as they see God in this way.

Questions 5-6. Encourage group members to write down their responses to these questions either before or during discussion so that they can use them for question 8.

Questions 7-8. Give participants time to respond to these questions as one exercise. You will have an opportunity to read these psalms to one another at the end.

Question 9. Encourage ideas about what you might do as a group to praise God together.

Question 10. Read your psalms of praise and join together in an expression of praise to God.